When I'm Gone

Organize Your Affairs Then Your Loved Ones Won't Have To

CHRIS FAIRWEATHER

Please note: This book is not designed to take the place of a will. Making a will is essential for all the really important stuff. This book helps with everything else.

Published by Berhampore Press
Wellington, New Zealand.
All rights reserved
Copyright 2018
BerhamporePress@gmail.com

ISBN-13:
978-1544636092

ISBN-10:
1544636091

TABLE OF CONTENTS

Instructions	5
First Things First	7
Who has possession of your last will and testament?	7
Executor of will:	7
Power of attorney:	7
Biographical Information	9
Personal Information:	9
Eulogy Help – Highlights of My Life	11
Medical information	13
Doctors and Specialist	13
Current Medications:	13
Your views on life support:	13
Caring for my Dependents	15
Care of My Pets	17
Business Interests	19
Property	21
Insurance detailsin	23
Bank Account Details	25
Automatic payments to stop	27
Deposits & Bonds	29
Investments and Shares	31
Broker or trading platform	31
Other investments	31
Pension Plans & Annuities	33

Credit & Debit Card Information	35
Debts / Mortgages / Loans	37
Tax and Social Security Information	39
Tax Numbers:	39
Social Security Number:	39
Who Normally Does Your Tax?	39
Other Tax Information:	39
Vehicle Details	41
Donations to Make on My Behalf	43
Items of value and who gets what	45
Memberships and Organizations to Notify of My Death	49
Internet & Utility Service Providers	51
Other notes on service providers:	51
Email and Social Media Details	53
After My Death	55
About my funeral	57
Please Invite these People to My Funeral	59
Special message to mourners	65
Last Wishes	67
Words of Wisdom for Friends & Family	69
Information for Friends and Family	71
Remember to keep this book up to date.	75

INSTRUCTIONS

This easy-to-complete book is an excellent place to gather useful information your friends and family will need once you've gone.

It provides a place to list information such as bank account numbers, insurance details, regular payments, personal information for funeral planning, and much more.

Make life easier for those you leave behind. They will certainly appreciate it — especially, as in their grief at your passing, they may overlook important things you'd like them to do.

Important Note: This book is not designed to take the place of a will. If you don't already have a last will and testament we suggest you get one drawn up as soon as possible. This book is designed to give additional information and clarity to those you leave behind. Having a will is the most important thing you can do to help loved ones left behind, this book comes a close second.

For your security, this book does not include a dedicated page for passwords. However if you want to put passwords into this book, and you have a safe person to leave it with, there are blank pages inside that can be used for this purpose.

Use this space for additional notes

FIRST THINGS FIRST

Who has possession of your last will and testament?

Name:

Address:

Phone: Email:

Executor of will:

Name:

Address:

Phone: Email:

Power of attorney:

Name:

Address:

Phone: Email:

Use this space for additional notes

BIOGRAPHICAL INFORMATION

Personal Information:

Date of birth:

Place of birth:

Mother's name:

Father's name:

Sibling's name/s:

Other significant relatives:

Use this space for additional notes

EULOGY HELP – HIGHLIGHTS OF MY LIFE

Here is a place to note the schools you've attended, places you've worked, your various achievements, important causes you've supported, and the relationships/marriages you've had over your lifetime that you'd like mentioned during your eulogy.

Use this space for additional notes

MEDICAL INFORMATION

Doctors and Specialist

Doctor's Name:

Contact Details:

Specialist Name:

Contact Details:

Current Medications:

Your views on life support:

Use this space for additional notes

CARING FOR MY DEPENDENTS

This is the place to make note of any special instructions in regards to any children or other dependents you have.

Use this space for additional notes

CARE OF MY PETS

This is the place to make note of any special suggestions you have in regards to your pets and who you'd like to look after them when you are no longer around.

Use this space for additional notes

BUSINESS INTERESTS

This is the place to make note of any business interests you have and how you would like these interests looked after. The main details of your businesses should be in your will, but here you can note details of a more personal nature.

Use this space for additional notes

PROPERTY

This is the place to make note of any property you own. The main details regarding who you are leaving your property to should be in your will, but here you can note details of a more personal nature such as trees you've planted and when, or details about your neighbors, their names and contact details. If you are renting note the name and contact details of your landlord.

Use this space for additional notes

INSURANCE DETAILS
(HOUSE, CAR, LIFE)

Here is the spot to list your insurance policies for your car, house, and life. Note provider details and policy numbers.

Use this space for additional notes

BANK ACCOUNT DETAILS

BANK:
BRANCH:
ACCOUNT NUMBER:

BANK:
BRANCH:
ACCOUNT NUMBER:

BANK:
BRANCH:
ACCOUNT NUMBER:

BANK:
BRANCH:
ACCOUNT NUMBER:

BANK:
BRANCH:
ACCOUNT NUMBER:

BANK:
BRANCH:
ACCOUNT NUMBER:

Note any automatic payments for memberships or subscriptions that will need to be stopped here:

Use this space for additional notes

AUTOMATIC PAYMENTS TO STOP

List the various automatic payments that your executor will need to stop.

1.

2.

3.

4.

5.

6.

7.

8.

10.

Use this space for additional notes

DEPOSITS & BONDS

DEPOSIT OR BOND:
DETAILS:
VALUE:

DEPOSIT OR BOND:
DETAILS:
VALUE:

DEPOSIT OR BOND:
DETAILS:
VALUE:

DEPOSIT OR BOND:
DETAILS:
VALUE:

DEPOSIT OR BOND:
DETAILS:
VALUE:

DEPOSIT OR BOND:
DETAILS:
VALUE:

DEPOSIT OR BOND:
DETAILS:
VALUE:

DEPOSIT OR BOND:
DETAILS:
VALUE:

Use this space for additional notes

INVESTMENTS AND SHARES

If you have a sharebroker or use a trading platform, here is the place to note the details, account numbers, and login details.

Broker or trading platform/s

Other investments

INVESTMENT:
DETAILS:
VALUE:

INVESTMENT:
DETAILS:
VALUE:

INVESTMENT:
DETAILS:
VALUE:

INVESTMENT:
DETAILS:
VALUE:

INVESTMENT:
DETAILS:
VALUE:

Use this space for additional notes

PENSION PLANS & ANNUITIES

Here is where you list details of your pension plan and annuities and any other income source that your executor will need to sort out.

Use this space for additional notes

CREDIT & DEBIT CARD INFORMATION

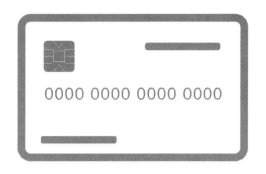

BANK & BRANCH:
CARD TYPE:
CARD NUMBER:

BANK & BRANCH:
CARD TYPE:
CARD NUMBER:

BANK & BRANCH:
CARD TYPE:
CARD NUMBER:

BANK & BRANCH:
CARD TYPE:
CARD NUMBER:

BANK & BRANCH:
CARD TYPE:
CARD NUMBER:

BANK & BRANCH:
CARD TYPE:
CARD NUMBER:

Use this space for additional notes

DEBTS / MORTGAGES / LOANS

Here is a place to list the debts, mortgages and loans you have. In this section include as may details as possible.

Use this space for additional notes

TAX AND SOCIAL SECURITY INFORMATION

Tax Numbers:

State:

Federal:

Social Security Number:

Who Normally Does Your Tax?

Name:

Address:

Phone:

Email:

Other Tax Information:

Use this space for additional notes

VEHICLE DETAILS

Include special instructions about care of vehicles, any hidden keys, and where registration and insurance papers are kept etc.

VEHICLE:

PLATE NUMBER:

INSTRUCTIONS:

VEHICLE:

PLATE NUMBER:

INSTRUCTIONS:

VEHICLE:

PLATE NUMBER:

INSTRUCTIONS:

VEHICLE:

PLATE NUMBER:

INSTRUCTIONS:

GENEROUS GIVING AWARENESS ASSISTANCE MISSION
SERVICES MORAL CARE AID
HELPING RESPECT
TOGETHERNESS
CHARITY LIFE VOLUNTEER TIME
ALTRUISTIC
COMMUNITY RESCUE DONATIONS
CONTRIBUTION SUPPORT HOPE TEAMWORK
ADULT ASSISTED PERSON

DONATIONS TO MAKE ON MY BEHALF

NAME OF CHARITY:
DONATION:

NAME OF CHARITY:
DONATION:

NAME OF CHARITY:
DONATION:

NAME OF CHARITY:
DONATION:

NAME OF CHARITY:
DONATION:

NAME OF CHARITY:
DONATION:

NAME OF CHARITY:
DONATION:

NAME OF CHARITY:
DONATION:

NAME OF CHARITY:
DONATION:

Note: Large donations should be mentioned in your will

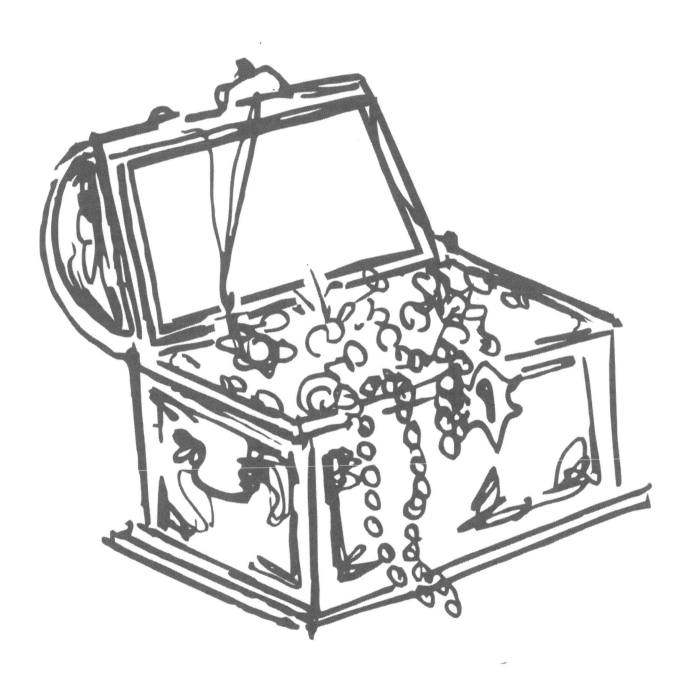

ITEMS OF VALUE AND WHO GETS WHAT

ITEM:
GIVE THIS TO:
CONTACT DETAILS:

ITEM:
GIVE THIS TO:
CONTACT DETAILS:

ITEM:
GIVE THIS TO:
CONTACT DETAILS:

ITEM:
GIVE THIS TO:
CONTACT DETAILS:

ITEM:
GIVE THIS TO:
CONTACT DETAILS:

ITEM:
GIVE THIS TO:
CONTACT DETAILS:

ITEM:
GIVE THIS TO:
CONTACT DETAILS:

ITEM:
GIVE THIS TO:
CONTACT DETAILS:

ITEM:
GIVE THIS TO:
CONTACT DETAILS:

ITEM:
GIVE THIS TO:
CONTACT DETAILS:

ITEM:
GIVE THIS TO:
CONTACT DETAILS:

ITEM:
GIVE THIS TO:
CONTACT DETAILS:

ITEM:
GIVE THIS TO:
CONTACT DETAILS:

ITEM:
GIVE THIS TO:
CONTACT DETAILS:

ITEM:
GIVE THIS TO:
CONTACT DETAILS:

ITEM:
GIVE THIS TO:
CONTACT DETAILS:

ITEM:
GIVE THIS TO:
CONTACT DETAILS:

ITEM:
GIVE THIS TO:
CONTACT DETAILS:

ITEM:
GIVE THIS TO:
CONTACT DETAILS:

ITEM:
GIVE THIS TO:
CONTACT DETAILS:

ITEM:
GIVE THIS TO:
CONTACT DETAILS:

ITEM:
GIVE THIS TO:
CONTACT DETAILS:

ITEM:
GIVE THIS TO:
CONTACT DETAILS:

ITEM:
GIVE THIS TO:
CONTACT DETAILS:

ITEM:
GIVE THIS TO:
CONTACT DETAILS:

ITEM:
GIVE THIS TO:
CONTACT DETAILS:

ITEM:
GIVE THIS TO:
CONTACT DETAILS:

ITEM:
GIVE THIS TO:
CONTACT DETAILS:

ITEM:
GIVE THIS TO:
CONTACT DETAILS:

ITEM:
GIVE THIS TO:
CONTACT DETAILS:

ITEM:
GIVE THIS TO:
CONTACT DETAILS:

ITEM:
GIVE THIS TO:
CONTACT DETAILS:

Use this space for additional notes

MEMBERSHIPS AND ORGANIZATIONS TO NOTIFY OF MY DEATH

ORGANIZATION:
CONTACT NAME:
PHONE OR EMAIL:

ORGANIZATION:
CONTACT NAME:
PHONE OR EMAIL:

ORGANIZATION:
CONTACT NAME:
PHONE OR EMAIL:

ORGANIZATION:
CONTACT NAME:
PHONE OR EMAIL:

ORGANIZATION:
CONTACT NAME:
PHONE OR EMAIL:

ORGANIZATION:
CONTACT NAME:
PHONE OR EMAIL:

ORGANIZATION:
CONTACT NAME:
PHONE OR EMAIL:

ORGANIZATION:
CONTACT NAME:
PHONE OR EMAIL:

INTERNET & UTILITY SERVICE PROVIDERS

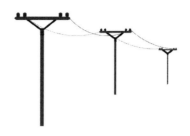

COMPANY:
ACCOUNT NUMBER:
CONTACT DETAILS:

COMPANY:
ACCOUNT NUMBER:
CONTACT DETAILS:

COMPANY:
ACCOUNT NUMBER:
CONTACT DETAILS:

COMPANY:
ACCOUNT NUMBER:
CONTACT DETAILS:

COMPANY:
ACCOUNT NUMBER:
CONTACT DETAILS:

COMPANY:
ACCOUNT NUMBER:
CONTACT DETAILS:

COMPANY:
ACCOUNT NUMBER:
CONTACT DETAILS:

Other notes on service providers:

Use this space for additional notes

EMAIL AND SOCIAL MEDIA DETAILS

COMPANY:
USER NAME:
PASSWORD:

COMPANY:
USER NAME:
PASSWORD:

COMPANY:
USER NAME:
PASSWORD:

COMPANY:
USER NAME:
PASSWORD:

COMPANY:
USER NAME:
PASSWORD:

COMPANY:
USER NAME:
PASSWORD:

COMPANY:
USER NAME:
PASSWORD:

Facebook: Delete or Memorialize? (please circle one)

Other notes on Social Media:

AFTER MY DEATH

Organ donation?   YES   NO   (please circle one)

If you circle YES you will need to make prior arrangements which will vary depending on which country you live in.

Blood type if known:

Burial or Cremation?   BURIAL   CREMATION   ECO   (please circle one)

Other:

Please bury me or spread ashes in this location:

Type of Funeral? RELIGIOUS   SECULAR   ECO   NONE (please circle one)

If religious please specify denomination:

Hymns/Music to play at my funeral:

1.

2.

3.

4.

Use this space for additional notes

ABOUT MY FUNERAL

If you have any special requests regarding the style of funeral, favorite flowers, setting or other items please note them here.

Use this space for additional notes

PLEASE INVITE THESE PEOPLE TO MY FUNERAL

NAME:
ADDRESS:
CONTACT DETAILS:

NAME:
ADDRESS:
CONTACT DETAILS:

NAME:
ADDRESS:
CONTACT DETAILS:

NAME:
ADDRESS:
CONTACT DETAILS:

NAME:
ADDRESS:
CONTACT DETAILS:

NAME:
ADDRESS:
CONTACT DETAILS:

NAME:
ADDRESS:
CONTACT DETAILS:

NAME:
ADDRESS:
CONTACT DETAILS:

NAME:
ADDRESS:
CONTACT DETAILS:

NAME:
ADDRESS:
CONTACT DETAILS:

NAME:
ADDRESS:
CONTACT DETAILS:

NAME:
ADDRESS:
CONTACT DETAILS:

NAME:
ADDRESS:
CONTACT DETAILS:

NAME:
ADDRESS:
CONTACT DETAILS:

NAME:
ADDRESS:
CONTACT DETAILS:

NAME:
ADDRESS:
CONTACT DETAILS:

NAME:
ADDRESS:
CONTACT DETAILS:

NAME:
ADDRESS:
CONTACT DETAILS:

NAME:
ADDRESS:
CONTACT DETAILS:

NAME:
ADDRESS:
CONTACT DETAILS:

NAME:
ADDRESS:
CONTACT DETAILS:

NAME:
ADDRESS:
CONTACT DETAILS:

NAME:
ADDRESS:
CONTACT DETAILS:

NAME:
ADDRESS:
CONTACT DETAILS:

NAME:
ADDRESS:
CONTACT DETAILS:

NAME:
ADDRESS:
CONTACT DETAILS:

NAME:
ADDRESS:
CONTACT DETAILS:

NAME:
ADDRESS:
CONTACT DETAILS:

NAME:
ADDRESS:
CONTACT DETAILS:

NAME:
ADDRESS:
CONTACT DETAILS:

NAME:
ADDRESS:
CONTACT DETAILS:

NAME:
ADDRESS:
CONTACT DETAILS

NAME:
ADDRESS:
CONTACT DETAILS:

NAME:
ADDRESS:
CONTACT DETAILS:

NAME:
ADDRESS:
CONTACT DETAILS:

NAME:
ADDRESS:
CONTACT DETAILS:

NAME:
ADDRESS:
CONTACT DETAILS:

NAME:
ADDRESS:
CONTACT DETAILS:

NAME:
ADDRESS:
CONTACT DETAILS:

NAME:
ADDRESS:
CONTACT DETAILS:

NAME:
ADDRESS:
CONTACT DETAILS:

NAME:
ADDRESS:
CONTACT DETAILS:

Use this space for additional notes

SPECIAL MESSAGE TO MOURNERS

If you have a special message you'd like read out at your funeral here is a good place to write it. Also make a note of who you'd like to read this message.

Use this space for additional notes

LAST WISHES

Make a list of last wishes that did not make it into your will but are important to you. This will help your friends and family pay a proper tribute to your life. Maybe it's that you'd like donations made to an organization rather than flowers. Or perhaps something personal.

Use this space for additional notes

WORDS OF WISDOM FOR FRIENDS & FAMILY

Make a list of those pearls of wisdom you've learned from a lifetime of experience. Or maybe write down a joke that resonates with you.

Use this space for additional notes

INFORMATION FOR FRIENDS AND FAMILY

Here are a few pages to make note of any additional information you want to pass on to your loved ones that we might have missed. It could be a secret chocolate cake recipe or the hiding spot for your stash of treasures. The more information you can provide your family, the easier it will be for them to deal with issues that arise durning the stressful time of your passing.

Use this space for additional notes

Use this space for additional notes

Use this space for additional notes

Remember to keep this book up to date.

If you don't already have a will, you should get one soon.
Why not phone for an appointment with a lawyer now?

Having a will is the most important thing you can do
to help loved ones left behind. This book comes a close second.

One last thing , please remember to tell friends
and family that you love them while you're alive.
It's too late once you're gone.

Made in United States
Orlando, FL
01 December 2024